MW01148010

Better Baby Sleep: A Handbook for Parents

by

Jane Stockly, M.S.

Illustrated by Ellen Surrey

Cover photo by Chemistry / Getty Images

"Better Baby Sleep: A Handbook for Parents"

Lulu Edition

Copyright © 2010 by Jane L. Stockly, M.S.

ISBN: 978-0-557-64562-6

Information about "Better Baby Sleep"
is available at the author's website:

www.betterbabysleep.com

Table of Contents

Chapter 1: For Parents and Caregivers

Parents, this book is designed to help you understand your baby's sleep. It provides important facts on infant sleep safety, as well as researched information that will help you develop the best way to manage your baby's sleep and encourage even breast fed babies to learn to sleep through the night. It has been my experience in parent education that chronic, unresolved sleep issues can lead to severe sleep deprivation, which can be a formidable barrier to healthy parent/child bonding and the general enjoyment of parenthood.

There are no surefire solutions that guarantee a baby will get a good night's sleep. I do not propose "no-cry sleep solutions," or recommend letting every child "cry it out." I do not offer any magical remedies. Your baby's sleep is something you as a parent will have to learn how to handle, based on your knowledge, experience and your family.

Each baby is unique, and every family is different, with varying lifestyles and ideas about which strategies they feel comfortable implementing. You may have other children to care for, who have their own needs to be considered along with those of the baby. With the scientifically researched, practical information presented here, you should be in a position to better manage your family's sleep needs and feel more confident in your ability to care for your baby.

Before she is able to sleep through the night, your baby needs to learn to self-soothe, to settle herself down to sleep without your help. Once she has learned to self-soothe, when she wakes up in the night, she will be able to fall back to a sound sleep on her own, without disturbing you.

When your baby sleeps a good portion of the night, this means you and your baby can both get enough rest and won't be so tired. Lack of parental sleep impacts not only the parents' sense of well-being, but also the way they interact with the baby; with other family members and particularly with any other children the parents may have. Excessive maternal tiredness can contribute to postnatal depression. When you are less tired, you may find you are able to enjoy your baby more and find bonding easier. A well-rested baby is usually in better spirits than one who is sleep-deprived, and the same holds true for a well-rested parent.

I am a parent of two daughters, both now in college. I know how tiring and how all-consuming it is to care for a baby 24 hours a day, seven days a week. I currently work as a parent education instructor at Glendale Community College in California; a program where parents from a variety of cultures and backgrounds bring their children, newborn to five years of age, to a child-friendly classroom environment, where they learn about child development and discuss various parenting issues.

Parents in my classes were the inspiration for this book. I have found that whatever their background, parents are often confused by all the information that is available on infant sleep, some of which is contradictory, culturally biased, and sometimes even judgmental. While some parents may not have any worries about getting enough sleep at night in this stage in their parenting, others are desperate for straightforward advice that will help them develop healthy sleep patterns in their babies and give them a chance to sleep undisturbed for a few hours at night. I know this, because every semester we welcome a new batch of sleep-deprived parents, many frazzled after breast-feeding their babies around the clock.

At our parent education program, I have often been asked to teach a special session on infant sleep for other teachers. One day while I introduced my lesson for encouraging sleep at night, I noticed one exhausted mother sitting back in her chair with her arms crossed, shaking her head in disagreement. She said she believed mothers who breast-fed could not possibly expect their babies to sleep well. After I replied that I exclusively breast-fed both of my babies, and that starting about three months of age they usually slept uninterrupted from 10 p.m. until 6 a.m., I had her attention for the entire sleep lesson.

A few months later I taught that class again, and the same mother was there, looking well-rested and cheerful, "I remember you, you're the Sleep Lady," she said as soon as she saw me. "You were a big help. I'm having a great time with my baby. I'm still breast-feeding and she sleeps through the night."

Her experience sums up the purpose of this book. I want all parents to have a great time with their babies and to form wonderful attachments with them, which are at the core of healthy child development. I think this is more likely if everyone gets the sleep they need.

I have worked with families and young children in varying capacities for close to 30 years. I hold a Nursery Nursing Diploma, from the United Kingdom; an Associate of Arts Degree in Social Science, from Glendale Community College; and a

Bachelors Degree in Human Development, from Pacific Oaks College. This book is the culmination project of a Master of Science Degree in Family and Consumer Sciences, from California State University Northridge (CSUN), where my focus was Family Studies and Parent Education. "Better Baby Sleep" is a product of research and study, combined with knowledge I have gained through years of practical experience. Here it is, as short and sweet as I can make it. I hope it helps.

Chapter 2: The Ability to Self-Soothe

The key skill your baby has to master to develop good sleep habits at night is the ability to self-soothe himself to sleep. This means he learns to relax and fall asleep without anyone being there to help him. Then, when your baby has matured, at around four months, if he has the potential to sleep for longer periods, he can self-soothe in order to link two sleep cycles together, sleeping longer stretches. A sleep cycle in an infant lasts about four hours. For a baby to sleep from six to eight hours at a stretch, he must link two sleep cycles together. A few babies are able to link three sleep cycles together, sleeping 10 to 12 hours at a stretch (*see Infant Sleep Cycles, page 14*).

Research shows that if parents have actively worked on laying infants down in bed before they are fully asleep, starting between the ages of six weeks and three months, their babies are more likely to self-soothe, cry less, and sleep better at night. For some infants, learning to self-soothe will be easier than for others. The first step, as soon as you notice your baby is not falling asleep while feeding, is to lay your baby down to sleep while she is still a little awake. Usually you'll notice this sometime before she has reached three months of age. If your child is older and has not learned how to self-soothe it is not too late to start; just expect the process to possibly take longer.

Babies can self-soothe to sleep in a variety of ways, from sucking fingers and thumbs to stroking the sheet they are lying on. Some babies may move around making rhythmical motions as if rocking themselves to sleep. Others vocalize to themselves, either in a calming way or in a way that may sound like they are "complaining." Every baby is unique and will figure out what works for him or her.

At bedtime or naptime, you may enjoy rocking your baby (a delight of parenthood), but try not to rock your baby all the way to sleep. Rather than holding or feeding her until she falls asleep, lay your baby down to sleep in her own space when she is drowsy but still awake. If you put her in her bed while still awake from early on, she is less likely to fuss about it. She may wiggle around, wave her arms, make a few sounds, etc., in order to find her comfort zone, but she will learn that her bed is a welcoming, safe place where she can relax and fall asleep. At first, there will be times she falls asleep before you have a chance to lay her down; at other times, she may refuse to settle down, in these cases you may need to actively calm her. Laying your baby down while drowsy, but awake, is something you can slowly begin introducing. Once she is snug in her bed, that does not mean you have to leave her side straight away, but you can gradually withdraw your attention. My husband remembers really enjoying his "goodnight" interactions with our daughters, when they were sweetly sleepy in their crib, but still just a little awake.

Babies Who Find Self-Soothing Difficult

Some babies are able to self-soothe effortlessly; however, others may find it more difficult and will complain and cry. Always talk to your pediatrician if you have any concerns. You should be keeping your baby's doctor fully informed about your baby's sleep. Those babies with more advanced motor skills for their age may find it harder to settle. Others may learn to self-soothe once they can control their hands well enough to be able to suck on fingers, etc. When your child is teething or feeling uncomfortable for any reason, do not expect them to self-soothe easily. There are even a few babies who just never seem to master this skill very well, who require extra effort, support, and patience from their parents. Occasionally, just the passage of time may bring about a better night's sleep for everyone, as is the case with colicky babies overcoming their fussiness (*see Colic, page 51*).

If your baby is having a hard time trying to self-soothe, he may not be tired enough for sleep, in which case you may keep him up for a while until he is a bit more tired. The opposite may also be true; he may be so tired and agitated that he is what I describe as "in overdrive," and cannot settle down on his own. If you think this is the case, you may lay him down to sleep earlier the next night before he reaches this point of over-exhaustion, and make sure he is getting enough opportunity to nap during the day (*see How Much Sleep Should My Child Get? page 26*).

If your baby becomes agitated, picking him up to calm him down and trying again to put him in bed may be the answer. Sometimes it takes a number of attempts, and a lot of patience, before success. There may be times when you decide to work on this another night, and finally hold him in your arms or rock him to sleep. What does not work one night may work another. Do not give up too easily.

Another strategy is to try to use something you notice your baby likes to your advantage. For example, a mobile hanging over the crib may give your baby something to focus on before drifting off to sleep. I once cared for a baby who seemed to love the sound of the vacuum cleaner (white noise). One night, after trying unsuccessfully to put her down to sleep for what seemed like the umpteenth time, I happened to remember this. I vacuumed her bedroom carpet and she immediately calmed down, falling sleep. She usually could self-soothe, but, whenever she would have a particularly hard time going down to sleep, out would come the vacuum cleaner, and it always helped. With my elder daughter, just taking her outside for a few minutes seemed to make all the difference in the world in helping her to calm down. For some babies maybe a light needs to be turned on or the radio played in the next room. Others may prefer darkness or silence.

Parents may even decide to give their babies space to complain and cry a little in order for them to figure out how to self-soothe. In some cases he may settle down within a few minutes or less. If you do this, you may want to time the length of the crying episode – sometimes a minute can seem like five when a baby is upset. If the baby gets more worked up and screams rise dramatically, this approach may be counterproductive with that baby. One couple I know timed their baby's bedtime cries and found the cries routinely lasted about the same time each night, and then he would be quiet. Some parents may be extremely uncomfortable with babies crying or complaining, so this may not work for them at all.

Only you and your partner can decide which strategies you are comfortable with and when to implement them. Ultimately, do what you feel is the right thing. Try to be creative in your thinking and, through trial and error, you may come up with a strategy all of your own.

Self-Soothing Strategies

Strategies that may help your baby learn to self-soothe at bedtime and naptime.

- Make sure she has all her needs met, she is not hungry, has a clean diaper, etc. Develop a bedtime routine that allows for special bonding time between you and your baby (*see Develop a Bedtime Routine, page 20*).
- Before laying her down in her own space, put her in the mood to self-soothe by cradling, rocking, and singing to her.
- Stay with your child for a while after putting her to bed, stroking her brow, using soothing words and singing, encouraging her to relax. Then slowly withdraw your attention

before she is fully asleep. You might still be singing as you leave the room.

- Try staying in the same room with your child while she falls asleep, but ignore her by pretending to be asleep yourself in your own space.
- If she is used to you being with her in order to fall asleep, have your partner try his or her hand at laying her down to sleep. Try going out for a little while to give them some quiet time together.
- Consider using a pacifier. Breast-fed babies should be more than one month old before using one.
- Allow your child to "complain" or even cry a little bit for a short time, as long as she is not hungry or in pain, etc. (*see Learn the Differences Between Your Baby's Cries, page 21*). Through this process, she may learn how to self-soothe if she is given the space to figure it out. Some babies fret a little before falling asleep.
- Try a "Comfort Item," when the infant is at least six months old, after the risk of Sudden Infant Death Syndrome (SIDS) has significantly dropped (*see SIDS, page 34*). Your baby may develop an attachment to a special stuffed toy or soft piece of material, which you can encourage. Developing a fondness for an object helps infants in their self-soothing processes, stroking a little soft toy while falling asleep, for example. Make sure that it is not overly fluffy, not too small (it cannot fit through a toilet roll tube), and is baby safe, as the possibility of suffocation and choking has to be considered. Large, stuffed animals are not safe for infants. Any piece of material or "baby blanket" should not be so big that it could cause strangulation or entanglement. If your child does have a preferred soothing item she likes to sleep with, you may wish to have a duplicate in case it ever gets lost or ruined. Realize once your child gets used to sleeping with something special, it may be hard for her to fall asleep without it.

Chapter 3: Developing the Ability to Sleep Through the Night

The ideal that many parents would like to achieve could unfold like this: After a relaxing bedtime routine, you lay your baby in his bed while he is still awake. After a moment, you tiptoe from the room, hearing familiar noises as he soothes himself to sleep. He moves from a light sleep into a deep sleep. After about three hours, he surfaces to a lighter sleep that may last about an hour, then self-soothes back down for another round of deep sleep. By linking sleep cycles, he sleeps for eight hours, or right through the night.

Infant Sleep Cycles

Infant sleep occurs in cycles, which alternate between periods of light and deep sleep. A baby will develop a sleep cycle lasting approximately four hours; about an hour of light sleep will be followed by two hours of deep sleep, followed by about another hour of light sleep. During deep sleep, the baby is hard to wake and has no eye or body movement. During light sleep, the baby is in a semi-alert state and easily aroused. His eyes, muscles, and head may move.

When babies wake up at night, it is generally from a light sleep, and, at first, it is usually because they are hungry. Their stomachs (about the size of their fists) need to grow large enough to hold more food so they can sleep longer periods.

It is when your infant has learned to handle the light-sleep periods and can self-soothe back down to a deeper stage of sleep without parental help (not being fed or held) that two, and eventually three sleep cycles may be linked together forming longer periods of sleep.

To self-sooth after waking between sleep cycles, your baby may suck his fingers, make noise, cry out, or self-rock in order to calm himself to the next sleep cycle.

Self-soothing, the ability to calm and relax oneself, is a wonderful and important developmental skill for your baby to learn, and is used throughout life.

Babies Got Rhythm!

For babies to sleep through the night they must learn to self-soothe, be able to link two or more sleep cycles together; their stomachs must grow to hold enough milk to last through the night and he or she must also develop their circadian rhythm. The circadian rhythm is the body's biological clock, which encourages more sleep at night than during the day. Each baby will develop according to his own unique, inner timetable; however, parents can take steps to promote development in these areas.

Circadian rhythm development begins in infants when darkness triggers the brain to release melatonin, a natural hormone that acts as a sedative. Daylight has the opposite effect, so exposure to indirect sunlight during the day, and darkness at night, promotes circadian rhythm development.

Help Your Baby Learn the Difference Between Night and Day

Once you feel able, begin taking your baby out for daily walks so he can get some daylight. This helps with the development of circadian rhythms, as if setting the baby's biological body clock.

At night, lay him down to sleep in a darkened room, and when caring for him during this time, avoid bright lights and too much stimulation through playing or excessive talking. Keep things very calm and low-key. Daytime is the fun time when you will encourage him to be more awake and active.

- Take your baby out for daily walks. Make sure your baby does not get too hot or cold and is not exposed to direct sunlight. Babies lose a lot of body heat through their heads, so if it is cold you may want to put a hat on her head.
- Going out for an hour every day, particularly in the afternoon, may help nighttime sleep develop.
- During the day, do your normal activities and do not feel you have to keep everything very quiet for the baby.
- Darken the bedroom sufficiently at night, making the room seem different from daytime.
- Room-darkening window coverings may help, particularly in the mornings when the sun first streams in, and during summer months when it gets dark later.
- Dim the lights and draw the shades as you prepare your baby for bed. Use a dim night-light during nighttime feedings to avoid turning on bright lights.
- Parents who have a later bedtime for their baby could keep household lights on a bit later until they begin the bedtime routine.
- Keep nighttime feedings as quiet and brief as possible. Regard nighttime feedings as being for sustenance only, while daytime feedings are much more social. Minimize play and talking to your baby at night.

Take Care of All Your Newborn's Needs

At first, feeding on demand and responding to your baby's every need will be your top priority. Directly caring for your baby and meeting all his needs for sleep, food, and comfort during the first few weeks of life will promote you and your partner's understanding and relationship with your baby, and your baby's understanding of you, too. Your baby will learn to trust and feel secure. Experts in childcare and development recognize the importance of building a rapport – a special bond – between you and your baby. Some parents feel this happens even before the baby is born; for others, soon afterwards; and for some, it may take some time to develop. The important thing to understand is that it does not matter if this bonding takes place before or after birth, as long as it happens. You will know when you have bonded with your baby. It is an incredibly wonderful feeling you have as you hold your baby close. My husband and I still have powerful memories of cradling our babies, even though they are now young adults.

If breast-fed, your baby will most likely wake up a little sooner to eat than those who are formula-fed. Newborns will often fall asleep at the breast or bottle and are fully asleep when laid down in their cribs.

Breast-feeding mothers should avoid falling asleep themselves while feeding, particularly while the baby is very young. I know of one family whose newborn suffocated at his sleeping mother's breast. Have someone monitor feeding if the mother is really tired.

Take extra care that your baby is comfortable before laying her down to sleep in a safe environment. All needs should have been met such as feeding and diapering. Did she have plenty of cuddles, is she warm enough, without being overly bundled or under-dressed? Expect to be feeding your newborn about every hour to every four hours. Babies' stomachs are small and need to be filled often. Time between feedings will gradually increase as the baby grows.

Swaddling an Infant

Some newborns like to be swaddled for lying down to sleep for the first couple of weeks, and may be helpful for babies with colic (*see Colic, page 51*). Swaddling probably replicates the familiar tighter space in the womb. Some swaddled babies may wriggle their arms out of the sheet as if they want a bit more room.

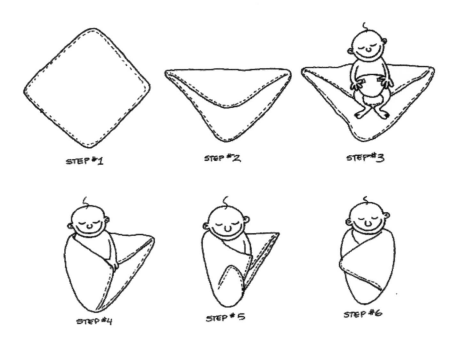

Lay Your Baby Down to Sleep While Still Awake

At some point your baby will not fall asleep while feeding. During the day, this is a good opportunity to spend time with your baby, showing him around the home and his environment, talking and playing with him for a while. He could have some "tummy time," which is when you lay your baby on his stomach so he may develop different muscles in his body. This may also help prevent him getting a "flattened" head from too much time spent lying in one position.

When it is time for sleep, make sure your baby is comfortable and begin to put him down in his bed when he is sleepy but still awake. By doing this, he has the chance to learn to calm and soothe to sleep in his own special way. Think of this as an important skill for him to learn, like crawling or walking. Some babies find this skill easier to master than others. Allowing him to fall asleep on his own without you or your partner being around will lead to him linking sleep cycles together with minimal disturbance for him or you.

Develop a Bedtime Routine

Familiar bedtime routines create soothing rituals that help your child get in the mood for sleep, and should be low-key and relaxing. These routines should develop as your baby grows by adding other activities over time such as reading a story, having a bath, or brushing teeth. Sitting your baby on your lap and reading to her can begin very early. These routines can be a useful tool throughout infancy as they encourage a child to settle down to sleep at the end of the day as well as giving you special bonding time together. Bedtime routines should not be rushed. A shortened version of the routine may be used before daytime naps.

From about six to eight weeks onwards, you can begin introducing a consistent pattern of calming activities leading to nighttime sleep, such as feeding and then changing the diaper (or the other way round), and rocking and singing to your baby before laying her down to sleep. Many babies enjoy listening to soothing music. Lullabies have been traditionally sung to encourage sleep in children. Songs are often handed down through the generations and make a nice addition to the bedtime routine. These songs can become very significant to your baby. I used to sing the Mary Poppins lullaby, "Stay Awake," to my children before they fell asleep every night. The first time one of my daughters heard that song in the middle of the day, she burst into tears. She so strongly associated that song with going to bed, she did not want to hear it when she was not ready for sleep.

Learn the Differences Between Your Baby's Cries

As you bond with your baby, and through some trial and error interactions during caring for your child, you will learn to distinguish differences in your baby's cries and body language. Babies cannot talk but use different cries to communicate their needs. You will learn that not all cries mean hunger. There will be cries for tiredness, pain, discomfort, or simply "I want to be held," and, of course, you will respond accordingly. One cry may be a "complaining" sort of cry, as she grouses about something that may be difficult for her. Understanding your baby's different cries will help you in meeting her needs appropriately and in deciding how to handle different situations. Some cries do not signal a need for immediate attention. Pay particular attention to the sounds your baby makes when put to bed and while learning to self-soothe.

Give Your Baby Some Space to Learn to Self-Soothe

From about six weeks onwards, when your baby wakes up at night, try not to rush to her side, but give her a little space and the opportunity to settle down by herself. Your baby could be sleeping in a crib within monitoring distance of your bed, and you will have begun to distinguish your baby's different cries and will be able to tell when she is hungry, in distress, or just "complaining" a little. When she is hungry or in distress, you should meet your baby's needs. If you think she is just complaining a little as she tries to make herself comfortable, you may want to leave her a bit to see if she can settle down back to sleep on her own. This delay gives her the opportunity to figure out how to calm and self-soothe. Self-soothing is a skill that, when developed, will lead to less disrupted nighttime sleep for her, for you, and for your family. After reading an early draft of this booklet, one mother chose to not pick up her six-week-old baby immediately when she awoke during the night, but stood by her crib and watched to see what her daughter would do. The very first time she tried this, to the mother's amazement and delight, after some shuffling around and making a few noises, her baby fell back to a deep sleep without any intervention, and slept longer.

Some parents choose to move their older babies into a separate room close by, once the risk of SIDS has lessened at six months (*see Sudden Infant Death Syndrome, page 34*). They can listen for any signs of distress in their babies, but not be disturbed by any minor noises they make through the self-soothing process.

In my own experience, one of my babies happened to be a particularly noisy sleeper. She would be sleeping soundly while I was kept awake listening to her. When I moved her into a nearby room, with doors left open and still within monitoring distance, I was able to sleep better.

If you are sharing the same room as your baby, one strategy that may help is to pretend to be asleep yourself, modeling what you would like your baby to do. Of course, if her complaints turn into signals of greater distress, you may wish to attend to them.

Don't Rush to Feed Your Baby at Night

As your baby matures, if she does not begin to start stretching the time between feedings at night naturally, encourage her to increase the time between nighttime feedings yourself. If your baby is eating every one to two hours around the clock, was not born prematurely, and is at least three weeks old and thriving, you could start to gradually stretch the time between feedings. The aim is to delay feeding when she wakes at night, and dissociate waking from feeding. For those who bottle-feed, there is a built-in delay as the formula is prepared. Use changing the diaper, patting, carrying, etc. to delay giving milk. (If you use changing the diaper for delay purposes, be aware you may have to change the diaper again after feeding.) Extending the feeding delay should be done very slowly – initially by five or ten minutes. After a week or two, the gap between feedings may become noticeably longer. Possibly two to three hour stretches in-between and your baby will start to sleep for longer periods at night. If not, be patient and persistent. This will happen naturally. It may take a little longer for some breast-fed babies, but the feeding delay is important.

As your baby gets closer to three months of age, make sure you are not in the habit of feeding her every two hours at night. Gradually stretch the time between nighttime feedings to at least four hours or more if you can. If your baby has been asleep for a few hours, waking him for a feeding just before you go to bed may help delay the next feeding so it does not occur in the early hours of the morning. Partners or other household members can be very useful in helping in the delaying process.

A Special Note for Breast-Feeding Mothers

If you are a breast-feeding mother, try not to fall into the trap of always responding to your baby's cries by putting a breast in his mouth, an easy habit to get into since babies do feed so often at first. Figure out his different cries and their meanings. Not all cries mean hunger. If he is just complaining or is a little restless, he can begin to learn to self-soothe. Partners can be very helpful during this time too; since they do not suckle your baby, they can try other calming methods. More importantly, your baby will know there is no suckling available, and that may help him break his reliance on your presence at night if that is what he is accustomed to.

Some parents believe if you breast-feed you need to sleep in the same bed with your baby. I have noticed it is the mothers who are bed sharing who seem to be feeding their babies every hour or two, for a prolonged period of time. Bed sharing may make breast-feeding more convenient, but it is harder to implement the delays needed to lengthen the time between feeds at night. Your breast is right there, readily available, and she may latch on to feed whenever she wants. This may result in your baby becoming a habitual "snacker," taking very small amounts of breast milk more frequently, even though her stomach has grown to be able to handle a larger quantity. I think one of the reasons bottle-fed babies tend to sleep better is that there is a "built-in" delay to feeding as the parents prepare the formula.

For your baby to feel satisfied for a reasonable period of time after eating, she needs to drain the whole breast, as the last part of the milk, the hind milk, contains the most fat and is more filling. The breast is usually drained after about ten minutes of solid sucking; for a newborn, it may take about 20 minutes. You will learn to feel when your breast is empty. Ideally, she will drain both breasts during each feeding, but draining one is better than just feeding a little from each side. Alternating the side you begin to feed on is a good idea. As her appetite increases as she grows, your breasts will respond by making more milk. As she gets older, she will become a more efficient eater, her jaw muscles getting stronger so she can suck more vigorously.

To successfully breast-feed while not sharing a bed with your baby means either you or your partner will have to get out of bed to pick up the baby, and then return him to his crib after feeding. It may mean more physical exertion and a slightly longer disruption of sleep in the short term, but as your baby gets older this natural delay in the beginning of feeding should encourage the lengthening of time between feeds so you can get more rest. You can feed either in bed or from a comfortable chair. Try not to fall asleep yourself. Remember partners can be involved through monitoring, bringing the baby to the mother, changing diapers when appropriate, and returning the baby to his crib.

Chapter 4: How Much Sleep Should My Child Get?

The sleep table, below, indicates how much sleep your baby may need over a 24-hour period. The hours given include naps as well as nighttime sleep. Remember, each child is different and the numbers shown are just averages. Some children may need more or less sleep than this. Generally, if your child is functioning well during the day, is active, and is usually in good spirits, and is achieving developmental milestones, he is probably getting his sleep needs met.

Age	Hours of Sleep per 24 hours
0 to 2 months	16 to 18
2 to12 months	13 to 15
1 to 3 years	12 to 14
3 to 4 years	11 to 13
5 years and up	10 to 11

Follow your baby's lead in determining his sleep needs. You may want to track the amount of sleep your baby is naturally getting over a 24-hour period if you are not sure these needs are being met. While researching this book, I got a phone call from a parent of a six-month-old at her wits' end over her baby not sleeping well. He was waking up about every hour at night. I asked her how long her baby slept during the day, and she replied that since she was working on her baby sleeping longer stretches at night, she allowed him to nap for only ten minutes at a time during the day. Clearly, that strategy made everything worse. Six-month-old babies, even if they sleep well at night, generally need two daytime naps (lasting much longer than ten minutes each) to meet minimum sleep requirements. This baby was so sleep deprived that it was impossible for him to soothe himself at night. I used the sleep table on the previous page as a guide for helping the mother to understand how her baby's sleep needs were not being met, so she could rethink her strategy.

Chapter 5: Sleep By Age

Below is an overview of how sleep patterns develop in a healthy full-term infant, and approximate ages when they may occur. Keep in mind, however, each baby is unique: some may take a little longer to enter the next stage. Those babies who are fed breast milk typically have closer feeding times at first, so feeding times may stretch at a slightly later date than for formula-fed babies.

Newborn Infants to Three Months

Newborns sleep about 16 to 18 hours per 24 hours, waking up every one to four hours to feed. Sleep periods are equally divided between day and night. Breast-fed babies usually go shorter stretches between feedings than those who are formula-fed, because breast milk contains less fat than cow's milk and tends to be digested more quickly than formula. The newborn baby will often fall asleep while feeding. Always lay babies down for sleep on their backs.

Newborns should be attended to whenever they demand it. Doing this for about the first three months has been found to minimize fussing and crying. More importantly, you are also building a close bond and pattern of trust between you and your child.

From six weeks of age onwards, you could begin laying your baby down for sleep while she is sleepy, but still a little bit awake, so she may begin to develop her own special way to self-soothe herself to sleep. You may start this when you notice she is still awake after feeding.

Newborn circadian rhythms (biological day/night body clock) are immature, so their sleep patterns are erratic at first, but the circadian rhythm will develop over the first three months. (*See Circadian Rhythms, page 16*).

At around two months, sleep patterns begin to shift with periods of sleep becoming longer. A preference for nighttime sleep begins to develop.

About one in five infants will develop colic between two and four weeks of age. Colic is excessive crying for prolonged periods of time with no apparent cause. The baby is regarded as "very fussy." See a pediatrician if you think your baby may have colic.

Colicky babies are healthy and gaining weight. Some babies with colic seem to be fussy all the time, while others may have crying concentrated around the late afternoon or evening hours, beginning about the same time each day. This latter colic crying pattern is similar to the crying pattern of non-colicky infants, as there is a tendency for many babies around the age of two months to be "fussy" during the late afternoon or early evening periods. The big difference between the two groups is the length of the crying bouts (*see Colic, page 51*).

Three to Four Months

At three months of age, infants' sleep will develop a more mature rhythm. The total length of time for daily sleep will decrease to an average of about 13-15 hours per day, as they have longer awake periods and longer sleep stretches too. Until the first birthday, 13-15 hours in a 24-hour period is most likely all the sleep needed. This amount of sleep is just an average, and there are some infants who will sleep more and some who will sleep less. Again, each child is different with varying sleep needs.

By three months of age, many infants will have sleep cycles lasting about three to four hours. If you have already begun laying your baby down to sleep while sleepy but still awake, she may have already learned to self-soothe and is linking two sleep cycles together, sleeping a stretch of about six to eight hours at night.

Four To Six Months

At four months, infants are more capable of putting two sleep cycles together, sleeping about six to eight hour stretches often between the hours of 10 p.m. and 6 a.m. Even though breast milk is quicker to digest than formula, many breast-fed babies are able to reach this milestone at this age too.

When babies are four months old, it is time for parents to set the long-term sleep habits they want their children to have if they have not already begun to do so. By doing this, parents may reduce the number of nighttime sleep interruptions in the future, as babies begin to develop particular sleep habits and associations connected with going to sleep. By this age, a baby should still be laid down to sleep while drowsy but awake, and not be allowed to always fall asleep while being fed or rocked, as she will develop a dependency, and only be able to fall asleep in these circumstances. She may then cry for a parent to come and help her fall into a deeper stage of sleep whenever she reaches that semi-alert stage of slumber. Rocking and holding your baby for songs, stories, comfort, and loving is a very important and special thing to do with your child and is a major part of the bedtime routine, but make sure she is snug in her bed before she closes her eyes for the night.

Also at this age decisions should be finalized on where the baby will be sleeping. If you have been sleeping in the same bed as your baby, discuss if this is something you and your partner want to do for the long term. Both of you should be in agreement on this issue. For some parents, bed sharing may be an enjoyable family experience and/or part of their cultural heritage, but for other parents babies come in bed only as a spur of the moment response to parental sleep deprivation (*see bed sharing and The Family Bed, pages 41 - 44*).

This age would be a good time to transition your baby to his own crib if you do not want to continue bed sharing. After this age, the longer you wait, the harder and more upsetting it will be for the child to make the change. Parents may want to think ahead about the potential effects of bed sharing, it could lead to less time for parental intimacy; lack of parental sleep and toddlers and preschoolers who may find it difficult to sleep without their parents, or are frightened to sleep alone.

Six to Eight Months

By six months, many infants are able to "sleep through the night," or sleep for around eight hours at a stretch. For example, a baby may sleep from 10 p.m. to 6 a.m., linking two sleep cycles. If your baby goes down to sleep at about 7 or 8 p.m. and wakes up in the small hours of the morning to be fed, you could try waking him for a final feed just before you go to bed yourself, somewhere between 10 p.m. and midnight. Listen for a light sleep period as an opportunity to wake the baby with minimal disruption of the sleep cycles. This strategy might mean he will not wake up for feeding after you have just fallen asleep. A few babies may even be linking three sleep cycles together, sleeping 11 to 12 hours per night, from about 7 or 8 p.m. to 6 or 7 a.m., for example.

By six months, you will have begun introducing some solid food to your baby's diet. Check with your pediatrician on how to go about this process. Usually the first food given is iron-fortified infant cereal. Offering this first food around supper time may help your baby sleep a little longer afterward, as solid foods take longer to fully digest than milk.

Naps will still be needed during the day in infancy. Many babies will fall into a pattern of having two naps per day, one mid-morning and the other sometime in the afternoon. Of course, this will depend on how their sleep is during the night. Remember, the average sleep requirement at six months is about 13 to 15 hours in a 24-hour cycle. Some may want more and others a little less. If they happen to sleep a good 12 hours at night, a baby may want just one nap during the day, usually taken after lunch.

Be aware that even those babies regarded as good sleepers will have occasional sleeping or settling down problems. Sickness, teething, and over-tiredness can cause distress and restlessness in your baby. Times of rapid cognitive or physical growth also make it harder for your baby to self-soothe and settle. Some parents feel that these settling problems result in their babies forgetting how to self-soothe, and they have to make an effort to encourage rebuilding this skill.

Eight Months to One Year

When infants are first learning to crawl or walk, more frequent awakenings can occur, as they have a harder time settling themselves after entering the light phase of sleep. Some babies may even pull themselves up to a standing position, holding onto the sides of the crib, and then have a hard time figuring out how to lie back down again. They will often call their parents for help.

Two naps a day are still the norm at this age, although a few may have just one, depending on if they sleep 10 to 12 hours at night. If your child is developing well, is active during the day, and is generally in good humor, she is most likely getting enough sleep.

One Year and Beyond

Children from one year to about three years of age have a biological need for an average of 12 to 14 hours of sleep per 24-

hour period. Remember, this amount will vary depending on whether your child has high, average, or low sleep needs. Between their first birthday and 18 months of age, about 90% of children shift to just one nap a day, often taken after lunch. If these naps run past 3 or 4 p.m., they may have an effect on what time your toddler will be ready for nighttime sleep.

The "ideal" bedtime is somewhere between 7 and 8 p.m., with a morning wake-up time of about 7 a.m. That may be impossible for many households to achieve, depending on parental work hours and daily schedules. Some parents may just prefer their children to have a later bedtime as they may sleep in longer in the mornings. Naps running past 3 or 4 p.m. may be needed for some children going to bed later than 8 p.m.

There is not a right or wrong time for bedtime. Each family should develop a set time when children are put to bed and which is adhered to most of the time. Occasionally, special situations may mean that routines change for a short time. The goal is for children and their parents to be getting enough rest over a 24-hour period so their biological sleep needs are met, and all can function well and enjoy their day. Over-tiredness often causes crankiness in both children and adults. Other points to consider in establishing a bedtime for your baby are time alone for yourself and time with your partner.

Between naps and nighttime sleep, your child should meet his sleep needs. Some toddlers may drop naps altogether as early as the second birthday, but generally children are at least three years old before this happens. Some parents may substitute a "quiet time" for afternoon naps, when children are encouraged to relax, play quietly by themselves, and look at books.

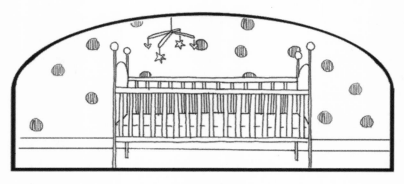

Chapter 6: Sleep Safety

The World Bank calculates the infant death rate in the United States to be 6.8 per 1,000, one of the highest in the developed world. Parents can take steps to reduce their baby's risks. The back-sleeping position must be used every time your baby is laid down for sleep: bedtime, nighttime, at home, away from home, in childcare, with a baby sitter or with relatives. It is also of critical importance to have a safe sleep environment for your baby. Infants die every year from being laid down to sleep in hazardous places. Babies can die from falling, entrapment, entanglement, wedging, overlaying and suffocation. Infant death rates from these causes have been rapidly increasing.

Sudden Infant Death Syndrome

Sudden Infant Death Syndrome (SIDS) is the unexplained, sudden death of an infant under the age of one year, usually occurring while the infant is sleeping. The thought of it naturally terrifies parents. I am guessing the majority of new parents spend some time hovering over their sleeping babies checking to see if they are still breathing. I know I did. When babies are in deep sleep, they can seem to be so still.

The risk for SIDS peaks in infants between the ages of two and four months, with death rates dropping significantly after six months of age. The chances your baby will die from SIDS are extremely low if the baby is a healthy full-term infant, if the mother was over the age of 20 during pregnancy, if she did not smoke while pregnant, and if the baby is not exposed to secondhand smoke. SIDS rates are higher among infants born prematurely.

Since 1992 SIDS death rates in America dropped approximately 50% as parents began to put their babies to sleep on their backs, following the "Back to Sleep Campaign" sponsored by the American Academy of Pediatrics (AAP) and the National Institute of Child Health and Human Development (*see Helpful Web Sites, page 68*).

American Academy of Pediatrics Infant Sleep Guidelines

In 2005, the AAP issued guidelines to reduce the risk of SIDS and sleep-related, accidental infant deaths, such as suffocation. Infants' re-breathing their own air has been determined to be the cause of some suffocation deaths. This occurs when a baby's nose and mouth have only a small airspace around them, because their face is either loosely covered or pushed up very close to something, stopping them from breathing in new, fresh air. The baby ends up breathing stale air they have already breathed out, loaded with higher levels of carbon dioxide and a lot less oxygen.

The following is based on AAP guidelines and should be taken very seriously by parents and anyone caring for an infant. These guidelines are based on careful, scientific research building on the lessons learned from actual cases where babies have died.

Babies must be placed on their backs when laid down to sleep. No side or stomach sleeping is recommended at bedtime or naptime. Tell this to everybody caring for your child.

Babies should sleep in their own space. This means separate from the parents or any other children, but close enough to be monitored. An infant crib, cradle, or bassinet that is certified by the Juvenile Products Manufacturer Association (JPMA) to meet current safety standards should be used (*see Helpful Web Sites, page 68*). Look for one of these symbols on the products:

JPMA Logo: Previous, left, and new.

In addition, check with the Consumer Product Safety Commission (CPSC) to see if there is a recall notice for any crib or baby product you intend to use, including those purchased new or used, or received as a gift (*see Helpful Web Sites, page 68*).

CPSC Logo

To prevent suffocation and entrapment, never put a baby to sleep on a waterbed, air mattress, sofa, or armchair, and never sleep with an infant in such a location. Babies may be brought into a parent bed for nursing, feeding, or comforting, but should be put back in their own crib before the parent falls asleep. At no time should an infant be brought into the parent's bed if the parent is using medications or substances that may impair their alertness or if the parent is very sleepy.

Babies should sleep on firm surfaces only. A firm crib mattress covered by a fitted sheet is ideal. Soft items such as pillows, comforters, quilts, or sheepskins should not be placed under infants. Soft, loose bedding and objects such as stuffed toys should not be put in the crib. If bumper pads are used, they should not be pillow-like, but should be thin, firm, well secured, and designed for that purpose. These should be removed before a child can pull himself up to a standing position.

Make the sleep surroundings safe. Remove all cords (such as from window blinds), ties, or strangulation hazards from around the sleeping area. If traveling and you are not sure of the sleep environment, consider taking an infant-safe, portable crib with you.

Babies should wear comfortable sleep clothing. There should be no head coverings. All-in-one sleeper outfits may be worn instead of having a blanket, as loose blankets may be dangerous. If blankets are used, they should be tucked in firmly, anchored under the foot of the mattress, and not reach up higher than the infant's chest. To prevent the baby wiggling down under the covers, he may be placed in bed with his feet touching the bottom of the crib.

The bedroom temperature should not be too hot or too cold. A lightly clothed adult should feel comfortable. Consider a thermostatically controlled, nonflammable heat source for maintaining a comfortable temperature in the sleep area. Avoid overheating the baby by not over-bundling. An infant should never feel hot to the touch or sweaty.

Do not expose your baby to any secondhand smoke. Never directly expose your baby or his environment to cigarette smoke. If you are a smoker, never exhale in your baby's face, even when not smoking, as your baby may breathe in toxins. Smoke outside and consider changing your shirt afterward, before holding your baby. Becoming a parent may be a good motivator to quit. Doctors are always willing to be supportive of this process.

Be a wary consumer. Avoid commercial products that claim they are designed to reduce the risk of SIDS, or state they keep a baby sleeping on their back. None have been fully tested to show efficiency or safety. There is no evidence that commercial electronic home monitoring systems reduce the risk of SIDS. Do some research before you buy any products. Use infant equipment that conforms to the safety standards of the Consumer Product Safety Commission (*see Helpful Web Sites, page 68*).

Pacifiers may be used. A pacifier may be used when putting a baby down to sleep but should not be reinserted once the infant falls asleep. Research shows pacifier use may reduce the risk of SIDS, although experts are not sure why. Pacifiers should not be forced on a baby, and must be cleaned often, replaced regularly, and never coated in any solution. For breast-fed babies, pacifiers may be introduced after one month.

The Safest Sleep Environment for Your Baby

Whether you're planning on designing a new nursery, or simply making space for a crib in your bedroom, you can create a safe and comfortable sleep environment for your baby.

The Room

The safest place for a baby to sleep is in a crib near the parents' bed. The AAP recommends a crib near the bed for at least the first few months of life.

- The room your baby sleeps in should be smoke-free, even when your baby is not there. Parents should not smoke and the baby should be kept away from people who are smoking. There should be no smoking inside your home. You should insist on a smoke-free zone around your baby.
- The temperature in the room should be comfortable, never too warm or too cold. If needed, I recommend the kind of thermostatically controlled portable heater that does not have an open heat source. The room should be comfortable for a lightly clothed adult.

- Room darkening curtains and/or blinds can be helpful in the summer, when it gets dark later and light earlier.
- There should be no cords from curtains or blinds anywhere near the crib, as these create a strangulation hazard.
- Any mobile or hanging decorations should be well out of the reach of a toddler standing up in a crib. Remember, your baby will grow! When your child reaches 35 inches (89 cm) in height, he has outgrown the crib and should sleep in a bed.

The Crib

Your baby's crib should meet CPSC safety standards and it should bear the JPMA logo, indicating that model has been tested and was found safe. You should also check the model at the CPSC website to be sure it has not been recalled. This is of particular importance if you are using an older crib or one that was purchased second hand (*see Helpful Web Sites, page 68*).

- For as long as you use the crib, it should have no loose, missing or broken slats and should have no missing or broken hardware.
- The width of the space between the crib's slats should be no more than 2 3/8" (60 mm, about the width of a soda can).
- The corner posts should be flush, or no more than 1/16 of an inch (1.5 mm) higher than the rails, headboard and footboards. Not all cribs have corner posts. If the corner post is more than 16" inches (40 cm) above the rails that is also acceptable.
- The mattress should be firm and designed for use with that crib.
- The crib's mattress should fit tightly in the crib. The mattress is too loose if you can fit more that two finger widths between the edge of the mattress and the crib side.
- The mattress should have a tight-fitting bottom sheet. Do not use an adult sheet with a crib mattress. Use a sheet that is made for crib mattresses.
- Do not use plastic bags or coverings on the mattress.
- There should be no pillows, quilts, comforters, sheepskins, stuffed toys, bumper pads, or any other soft, padded or plush products in the crib.

- Avoid devices, pads or wedges that prop a baby on her side, or claim to "prevent SIDS" and suffocation. These devices have not been tested to show if they reduce or increase the SIDS risk and have not been proven safe. The back sleeping position is the best way to minimize the risk of SIDS for your baby.

When you travel, you need to be prepared to create a safe environment wherever you go. If you're going to use cribs provided by hotels, ask them for the make and model number and check the CPSC website to make sure that their crib meets the standards and has not been recalled. If you are not sure of the sleep environment, consider bringing an infant-safe, portable crib along.

The Baby

When babies are sleeping they should be on their backs. If they are sleeping in a stroller, car seat or are placed in a baby carrier, make sure the baby is not in a scrunched position with their chins on their chests. Babies' airways are soft and necks should be extended when they sleep to ensure there is no compression of the airway.

- Your baby should sleep in a sleeper or similar sleep clothing, these are preferable to blankets.
- If you choose to use a blanket, use a thin blanket tucked snugly around sides and foot of the crib mattress. For sleep, place your baby on her back with her feet near the foot of the crib, so she can't slide down under the blanket. The blanket should reach only as far up as your baby's chest.
- Make sure your baby's head will always remain uncovered during sleep.
- Before putting your baby to sleep, remove any bibs, ribbons, necklaces and anything else that may cause a strangulation hazard.
- If you use a pacifier, do not use anything to tie it to your baby's wrist or neck.

- Avoid overheating. Your baby should not be sweating or feel hot to the touch, especially at the hands.

Babies are Not Adults

Sometimes when adults see babies sleeping on their backs, with no pillow or blankets, they may wonder if the baby is comfortable, since they themselves wouldn't be in that position or environment. Babies become accustomed to sleeping on their backs without soft pillows or fluffy padding, and they sleep quite comfortably that way. Some parents or caregivers may even decide not to use the back-sleeping position because they think it may increase the risk of choking or "it just looks awkward." The National Institute of Health found that back-sleeping babies have not been shown to have increased problems with choking; healthy babies automatically swallow or cough-up fluids. So don't be tempted to offer your baby a "cozy" comforter or pillow or lay them in another sleep position. This can be very dangerous for your baby. You should make sure that anyone caring for your baby understands this.

Maximizing Safety if You Sleep With Your Baby

Choosing whether or not to sleep in the same bed as your infant is a controversial topic. Those in favor of parents and babies sleeping in the same bed, "the family bed," say it promotes bonding and breast-feeding, and is a traditional practice carried out in many of the world's cultures. I believe parents can bond with their babies and breast-feed successfully with each sleeping in their own space.

The AAP recommends having babies sleep in a crib near their parents' bed. Adult sleep arrangements in Western cultures are dangerous for infants, and experts agree that the absolute safest sleep environment for an infant is in a crib or bassinet close enough to the parents' bed to be monitored. The AAP guidelines reflect the potential dangers of adult Western beds. Babies should be laid down for sleep in a crib near the bed.

Parents who smoke should never sleep in the same bed with their infants, as this may increase an infant's exposure to smoke components. Smokers, even when they are not actively smoking, exhale potentially harmful toxins that their babies breathe in when lying face-to-face with them in bed. Some European studies show direct contact with smokers increases an infant's risk for respiratory infection and SIDS.

For those who choose bed sharing, measures need to be taken to prevent infant suffocation, wedging, entrapment, strangulation, falling, or overlaying.

Baby-doll Illustrations from the Consumer Product Safety Commission

Below are photos of dolls depicting dangerous situations in order to show how hazardous adult beds can be for babies. In many cultures where bed sharing is customary, the mattress is placed directly on the floor and away from the wall.

A doll is used to illustrate the danger of furniture placed too close to an adult bed.

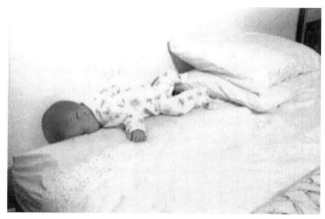

Here the doll illustrates the danger of a baby sleeping on an adult bed that is placed too close to a wall.

The doll shows how a baby can become trapped in an adult bed's footboard. Headboards and footboards are not built to the same standards as cribs and can be hazardous to an infant.

The Family Bed

If you feel strongly that you want to bed share with your baby, then here are some safety tips to consider:

- Bed mattresses should be firm and placed directly on the floor so babies cannot fall from a height. Sleeping directly on the floor is the norm in many world cultures that bed share.
- Bed mattresses should be pulled away from the wall and nearby furniture so there is no chance of an infant getting wedged between them.
- Use a tightly fitted sheet over the mattress.
- Remove all nearby clutter, and raise any hanging cords from blinds or curtains out of reach.
- Secure furniture, such as dressers, to the wall. This is particularly important if you live in an earthquake zone.
- The entire bedroom should be childproofed since it takes the place of the crib. Remember, babies learn to roll, crawl, climb, and walk sometimes sooner than we expect. Be prepared in advance.
- Headboards, footboards, and side rails should be removed (including those designed to prevent children from falling out of bed). These may entrap an infant.
- Remove any unsafe bedding and keep any pillows out of the baby's way and away from the floor around the bed.

Even if you follow all these steps, the safest place for your baby to sleep is still in a crib next to your bed. You may consider co-sleeping products. These are low-sided, bassinette-type baby beds designed to be placed directly in the parents' bed (a king-size bed may be needed to use these comfortably). These are only for newborns and infants unable to roll over. Before purchasing check-in with the Consumer Product Safety Commission to verify there are no reported safety problems connected with these co-sleeping products (*see Helpful Web Sites, page 68*).

Avoiding a "Flat-Headed" Baby!

When it is time for sleep, always lay your baby on her back in a safe sleep environment, but during the day, when she is awake, vary your baby's position. Have her lie on her stomach to prevent a misshaped head and to encourage muscle development and build strength.

Infants spend a lot of time lying on their backs while they are asleep. In the years since the AAP began recommending infants be put to sleep on their backs, there has been an increase in babies developing plagiocephaly, also known as positional molding of the head. The skull becomes flattened due to lying in the same position so much. If you have any concerns your child has an odd-shaped head or any flattened areas, you should discuss them with your pediatrician.

To prevent a "flattened head," vary your baby's sleep position by turning his head to different sides when you lay him down to rest, or place the baby with his head at the foot of the bed. Turning the crib around or changing its position in the room may help.

When your baby is awake, do not always have him in a sitting position, in a baby seat or car seat. Allow him to play on the floor. Place your baby on his tummy for supervised "tummy time" every day. This should be done from early on as babies not used to being placed on their stomachs may complain when they are a little older. You can try laying your baby on his tummy across your lap, or it may help for you to sit on the floor with your baby at first. You can then lay your baby across your legs on his stomach, so he can peek over your thighs. The baby's head will be raised slightly so he is better able to see any toy you may show him on the ground. Your baby may like some tummy time after a bath, when you can rub some baby lotion on his back and provide a gentle massage.

Another benefit of putting your baby on her stomach every day and varying positions is this helps her to strengthen and develop the different muscles in her body and encourages a full range of neck rotation. This promotes the optimum development of her motor skills, body control, and movement. Research indicates babies who are not placed in a variety of different positions, spending much of their time on their back, may be slightly delayed in learning how to roll, crawl, and walk.

Don't Panic if Baby Rolls Over in Bed

Sometimes, after you put your child down to sleep on his back, you may find him rolled over onto his stomach. If this does occur, you do not need to change his sleep position, which may wake him. If he has the ability to roll all the way from his back to his front himself, he has developed the strength and ability to cope with this position. Some babies even develop a preference for sleeping on their stomachs and may flip from their backs to their tummies before drifting off to sleep. But remember: always lay him down to sleep on his back, regardless of what sleep position he ends up in.

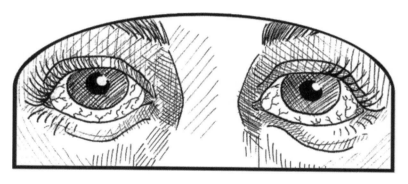

Chapter 7: Baby Has Trouble Sleeping?

All infants will wake up during the night at some point and have problems sleeping. Even babies who are usually very good sleepers and know how to self-soothe may sometimes revert to previous sleep patterns. Talk to your pediatrician about any concerns you may have.

Below are a few questions to ask yourself when your baby is having trouble sleeping and some possible answers and solutions:

Is your baby still so young that his body clock has not developed?

Be patient (*see Circadian Rhythms, page 16*).

Is your baby uncomfortable?

Is she sick or in pain, too hot or too cold? Does she need a diaper change? Is she teething? Do what you need to do in order to take care of those things.

Is she hungry? Did she get all her nutritional needs met during the day?

If she seems to need a feed in the early morning hours, consider waking her up for a feed just before you go to bed. Paying attention to her sleep cycles may help; if you are able to wake her up when she is in lighter sleep, she may be more inclined to eat sometime between 10 p.m. and midnight (*see Infant Sleep Cycles, page 14*).

Is your baby still feeding every one to two hours at night?

If your baby is at least three weeks old, try to delay feeding by changing the baby's diaper or using other tactics in order to stretch the time between feeds. Try resettling him in bed first if he is at least six weeks old, as he may not be hungry. Have your partner try settling him down (*see Don't Rush to Feed Your Baby at Night, page 22*)

Is your baby developing new motor skills?

Learning skills, such as crawling or walking, may mean he has a harder time than usual self-soothing. This means relaxing bedtime routines may last longer as winding down will be harder. Extra soothing words, or whatever calming activities your baby responds well to, may be needed during this period. Be as calm as you can, gradually withdrawing your attention.

Is your baby overtired?

Did she miss out on a nap or has she been going to bed later than usual? Do you need to make bedtime a little earlier or adjust a nap? Is she getting her sleep needs met? (*See, page 26, How Much Sleep Should My Child Get?*) Feeling overtired can make it harder to settle down. Children often have the habit of waking up about the same time each morning, even if they went to bed later than normal. Setting a regular bedtime that you stick to most of the time helps. The ideal bedtime is between 7 and 8 p.m. Bedtime may be later for some families, but whatever you choose, try to be as consistent as you can.

Is it hard for your baby to relax at the end of the day?

Avoid any rowdy activities close to bedtime such as exciting Daddy play (he can tone it down or read and sing instead). Limit TV viewing as well.

Do you have some sort of a bedtime routine?

Bedtime routines help children wind down at the end of the day for sleep and should not be rushed. Occasionally, a shortened version may be substituted if time is an issue. Do you need to enrich your current bedtime routine by reading or singing, etc.? Involve your partner in these, particularly if your partner has not been with your child all day. The bedtime routine is a wonderful opportunity for working parents to spend quality time with their children.

Is your baby active during the day? Does she get some outside time?

Add more physical activities such as "tummy time," playtime, walks in the park, etc.

Do you need to adjust naps or eliminate one?

Naps after 3 or 4 p.m. for older infants may cut into nighttime sleep if they go to bed between 7 and 8 p.m. Those going to bed later may need to rest into the late afternoon. Between one year and 18 months, most toddlers transition to one nap a day, usually taken after lunch.

Does your baby get attention during the day?

Are you or your partner able to spend quality time with your baby during the day? Many babies will prefer to be awake around their parents if they have not been with them during the day. If parents are feeling guilty about not being able to be with their children as much as they would like, it may be harder for them to give their babies the space needed to learn to self-soothe. If you are both away from your child during the day, spend quality time with her after work and on your days off. Quality time is time when you give all your attention to your child or actively include her in what you are doing. Quality time can be sharing a very relaxing, non-rushed bedtime routine together. Give plenty of cuddles and include your baby whenever possible in household tasks that have to be done. For example, if you are in the kitchen cleaning up, bring your baby with you, explain to her what you are doing, and have an ongoing interaction. Hand her different kitchen items to explore and play with that are baby safe.

Would it help to move your baby to another sleep location?

Either from your bed to a crib, or into another room close by, leaving doors open or installing a baby monitor so you can still hear and respond to your baby's needs. Sometimes the problem is not that the baby cannot sleep, but that the parents are so aware of every noise their baby makes while sleeping that they are the ones staying awake.

Colic

Colic is excessive infant crying and fussiness. The clinical researchers' definition is infant crying occurring for at least three hours a day, at least three times a week, for three or more weeks in a row. Colic is linked with sleep disturbances in an infant and has no known cause or cure, although researchers suspect it may be due to an immature nervous system. Colicky babies are in good health and gaining weight. If a pediatrician rules out all medical causes such as a milk allergy or digestive problem, a fussy baby has colic or is a "colicky baby."

According to the American Academy of Pediatrics, about one in five infants develop colic. Colic typically begins when the infant is between two and four weeks old, and slowly tapers off between two-and-a-half to four months of age.

The crying and general fussiness of colic may occur all the time, or in some babies may be concentrated around the late afternoon or early evening hours, beginning about the same time each day. Nobody has figured out why this is so, but for some reason it is common for many babies, those without colic as well, to be "fussy" around the late afternoon–early evening period, at about two months of age. The bouts of crying for the colicky baby are prolonged and the infant is unsoothable, even by feeding. The crying seems to begin and end without any reason, and while occurring, the baby will have clenched fists, an arching back, flushed skin, a distended abdomen and a distressed face.

There is no known treatment for colic. Colic will go away with the passage of time. Infants with colic suffer no long-term problems, but it can be very hard on the parents. If your baby has colic – hang in there!

Tips for Colic
- Visit your pediatrician for diagnosis of any physical conditions that cause fussiness and crying in your baby.
- Remember that colic is a very normal part of many parents' experiences. It is not your fault or your baby's.
- Passage of time helps. It will get better.
- Observe your child and experiment with different strategies to see if any help calm him a little.
- Carry your baby around in an upright position. Try using different carrying positions to find one that he seems to prefer. Using a baby sling or carrier may make it easier for you.
- Rock your baby, either in your arms or in a baby carriage or swing.
- Lay your baby over your lap on her stomach or along your arm.
- Have other relatives or friends help out. Take turns holding the baby.
- Sing. Play music.
- Play "white noise," such as the sound from a washing machine or vacuum cleaner. White noise may be recorded or bought on CD and can be very soothing for some infants.
- See if swaddling helps.
- Take your baby outside or even for a drive.

If your anxiety level is extremely high, and you become very tense and feel that you could even shake, squeeze tightly, or hurt your baby in any way, give your baby to someone else to hold. If no one is around to help, put your baby down in a safe spot such as a playpen or crib, and give yourself a break. Your baby will do just fine on his own for a while and it may even help. Tense parents may transmit these feelings to their babies, making it even harder for the babies to calm down.

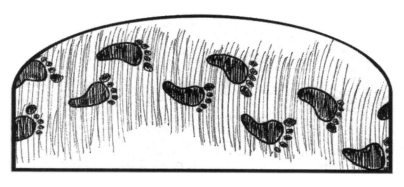

Chapter 8: Baby Steps to Better Baby Sleep

Here is a final summary of what you can do to maximize your baby's ability to sleep during the night in a simple step-by-step format.

Safety First

Always lay your baby down for sleep on his back every time you put him down to rest, and tell this to everyone who may look after your baby. Be sure to read the entire chapter on Sleep Safety (*page 34*) and discuss your baby's sleep with your pediatrician.

Day and Night

Help your baby learn the difference between daytime and nighttime (*see the section Help Your Baby Learn the Difference Between Night and Day, page 16*). As soon as you feel able, begin taking your newborn outside everyday for walks. Be active with your baby during the day and at night limit your interaction keeping things low-key and mellow. Develop a special nighttime routine that is soothing and involves your one-on-one attention such as reading stories and singing lullabies (*see Developing a Bedtime Routine, page 20*).

Make a Decision on Where Baby Will Sleep

Create a safe sleep environment for your baby. I recommend a crib within monitoring distance of your bed, and the American Academy of Pediatricians agrees. Be sure to read the entire section on the Safest Sleep Environment for Your Baby, *page 35, Sleep Safety*. If you choose to bring your baby into your bed do everything you can to minimize risk and read The Family Bed guidelines (*page 44)*.

By the time your baby is four-months-old think about your family's sleep arrangements. If your baby sleeps in the same bed with you and you do not want to continue this for the long-term, make the change to a crib now, as it will only be harder if you wait.

Gradually Delay Feedings at Night

Delay nighttime feedings perhaps by changing the diaper first. With bottle-fed babies a delay may already be built-in to the process of preparing the bottle. Delay by only a little at first and then gradually try and stretch the time between feedings.

Lay Your Baby Down to Sleep While She is Still Awake

When you notice your baby is not falling asleep during feeding, begin laying her down for sleep while she is drowsy but still a little awake. Do not always rock her to sleep.

Give her the space to figure out how to fall asleep on her own. Pay attention to how she reacts and what sounds she makes.

Give Your Baby Space to Fall back to Sleep

Once your baby is about six-weeks-old do not rush to pick him up when he calls for you at night. Give him a chance to self-soothe back to sleep. Learn the differences in your baby's sounds so you know when you need to respond more quickly and when you can let him be.

Trouble Self-soothing?

If your baby has trouble self-soothing read the section the Ability to Self-Soothe (*page 9*). Try staying in the room with the lights low and gradually withdrawing your attention or pretend to sleep yourself, reinforcing the concept of bedtime. Some babies may find it more difficult to learn to self-soothe and you may need to make more of an effort.

Chapter 9: All Kinds of Families

Families are at the heart of rearing children. Involving your partner, other family members, or friends in the care of your baby, such as bedtime routines, has huge benefits for the whole family and can help support your enjoyment of parenthood.

Single Parent Families

If you are parenting on your own, encourage involvement from the mother or father of your child whenever appropriate. Other adult family members or friends could be involved in your child's life and share in some of the childcare tasks when possible. Grandparents, uncles, and aunts can be a wonderful asset for you and your child. If you do not have a partner to share the responsibility of raising your child, then it is even more important you develop a network around you of caring, supportive adults, who both you and your child can rely on to be loving and helpful. Establishing healthy sleep patterns for both you and your child will help you function well as a family unit.

Fathers / Partners Are Important

Research shows that the more fathers/partners perform childcare tasks and play with their children, the closer the bonds between them. Bedtime routines and helping soothe a restless infant are childcare activities that partners can participate in. It not only helps them understand and learn more about their child, but also the child will get to know them better. Mothers can get some rest by sharing duties. How these duties are divided will be unique for each family, depending on work schedules, personality and skills, and other factors. The only thing a father cannot do is breast-feed. He may help diaper and bring the baby to the mother for feeding; bottle-feed with formula or expressed breast milk; burp, hold, and soothe the baby. Some families I know specifically choose a later bedtime for their children so the partners can be around to be involved with nighttime routines and spend time with them at the end of the day.

Encourage your partner to read this booklet. Sharing an understanding of infant sleep may help you come to a consensus on key issues such as bedtime, where the child sleeps, etc. In my experience, couples who can work as a team and talk through issues connected with their children generally feel more competent in being parents, and their children benefit. Also, they are less likely to suffer from too much sleep deprivation and related problems if they share the child-care responsibilities as much as possible and work to figure out strategies together to best accommodate their unique family situation and needs. Be aware that there can be different ways to do things in the same family, and, as long as it is not unsafe, doing things differently is often all right. Try to avoid correcting your partner all the time if they do not do tasks as well as you, and do not feel badly if they seem to do some things even better.

Multigenerational Families

Some grandparents and other relatives may not realize that babies must be laid down to sleep on their backs. About 30 years ago when I went through my Nursery Nurse training, we were taught to place babies to sleep on their stomachs. Times, and what is regarded as safe and developmentally appropriate child-care practice, change. Explain that the rate of SIDS has been reduced by 50% since we started putting babies to sleep on their backs.

Using Child Care or Family Care

Many parents use family members, friends, or childcare professionals to care for their children while they work. If someone other than you or your partner is caring for your baby, put time and energy into finding the best childcare situation that you can. Build up a good relationship and pattern of open communication with whoever cares for your child. Whether they are a family member or not, work as a team in the best interests of your child. Discuss, share, and write down any daily routines such as eating and sleeping, plus preferences you or your child may have. If you have a later bedtime for your child, have her take more naps or longer naps during the day if necessary.

Ask to see the location where your child will sleep, and make sure it is safe. Talk to your childcare provider about always laying your child down to sleep on his back. SIDS and infant suffocation can occur in day care settings as well as in the home. If your child has a favored item to self-soothe with, make sure that he has it everyday and that its use is respected by the caretaker.

If you are breast-feeding and you have the opportunity to have "lunch" with your baby, do so. Some mothers express milk to be fed via a bottle during the day, while others may use formula, and continue breast-feeding at home. You should be able to visit during the day whenever you want. Good infant child-care providers will encourage you to be around whenever possible.

Infant Care Centers

Infant care centers care for infants and toddlers under the age of three years and must adhere to state health and safety codes in addition to providing a warm and nurturing atmosphere for children. All states have health and safety codes to ensure the appropriate care of young children. In California, Title 22 regulates these centers.

Licensed Infant Care Center Health and Safety Codes

Below are some of the Title 22 requirements pertaining to infant sleep.

- Infant care centers need to develop, maintain, and implement a written plan to ensure the meeting of every baby's needs, including rest and relaxation.
- Parents should expect daily charting of their babies' eating and sleeping habits, as well as a record of bowel movements.
- All babies shall be given the opportunity to nap/sleep whenever they want without distraction or disturbance from other activities at the center.
- No infant shall be forced to sleep, to stay awake, or to stay in the napping area.
- Nap times may be flexibly scheduled by the center for only those children over the age of one year.
- A standard size crib or port-a-crib that conforms to safety standards must be provided for each baby who is unable to climb out of it. The mattress should be at the lowest position and the baby should be able to stand upright in it.

Chapter 10: Enjoying Parenthood

This book will hopefully give you the information you need to be able to understand and manage your baby's sleep, so you have a baby who can sleep through the night much of the time. This way you can get an adequate amount of sleep yourself and have the energy to fully enjoy being a parent. A parent who is rested can be more relaxed; a more relaxed parent usually has a more relaxed baby.

While taking a nap during the day can be beneficial for you when the baby is sleeping, daytime sleep quality is not quite as good as nighttime sleep quality, and does not fully compensate for nighttime sleep loss. If you feel so sleep-deprived that you are not functioning and coping well, try to have your partner or someone else come in to care for the baby for a few hours. Night is preferable, so you can try to get some sleep. A good eight hours of uninterrupted nighttime sleep might make all the difference in the world.

Being a parent is very demanding so take time out for yourself when you can to minimize your stress levels. Some of the activities suggested to help a baby sleep at night are also activities that may help you relax as well. Taking a baby outside for a walk, singing lullabies, and gently rocking not only soothe your baby but may be soothing for you too. Going for a walk is good exercise for releasing some built-up tension. It is difficult to sing lullabies well and remain anxious. Figure out strategies that help you relax. You need to be taking care of yourself so you are in the best shape possible to care for your baby. Also realize that there is no such thing as a perfect parent. Doing the best you can is usually good enough.

If you happen to have a colicky baby, doing the best you can is often all you can do. Try to remain as calm as possible. There is no known treatment, although you may figure out which strategies help a little. Remember, colic is neither your fault nor the baby's. Keep this in mind – this difficult phase will pass. Have other people take turns holding the baby if possible and, if the screaming makes you extremely anxious, it is all right to put the baby down in a safe place, such as a crib, and let them be on their own for a while. Doing this may be helpful in some cases. Sometimes, the more focus the parents give to trying to "fix the problem," the worse they can make it. This may be something the child just has to go through. There are no future ill effects from having colic as a baby. You and your child will get through this taxing challenge together and you will both really appreciate life without it when that time comes.

Sharing childcare duties and nighttime feedings with your partner is helpful if this is at all possible. Sending your partner in to manage an awake baby in the middle of the night when you normally do it can be invaluable in many ways. Prioritize your responsibilities. A well-cared-for baby takes precedence over a spotlessly clean house. Other family members or friends may be around who are more than willing to lend a hand. Paying for additional support, if you can afford it, may be useful.

Watch out for signs of postnatal depression and get help from your doctor and support network if needed. Maternal sleep deprivation has been linked with postpartum depression. Sleep deprivation makes it worse and in some cases may even create depression. Take care of your own sleep needs as much as you can. Establishing healthy infant sleep patterns will help a lot. Fluctuations in hormone levels are very normal for women after having a baby, so expect some mood swings, but if you ever find yourself feeling very depressed or having strange thoughts about harming yourself or your baby, talk to your doctor about it right away. There is treatment for postpartum depression. Also, any time you feel overwhelmed by your role as a parent, talk to your child's pediatrician.

Consider joining some sort of parenting group, such as a parent education program, where you can meet other parents with their babies and socialize together. Parenting is a tough job, and it can really help to have someone who is in the same situation as you to discuss things with, someone with whom you can share your questions, concerns, successes, and joys. Parents can learn a lot from each other as well as gain some much needed moral support. Having a child can be a great way to meet new friends, and your child may benefit from the friendships formed with other parents' children.

Time flies when you are a parent; when I think back to my early days of motherhood, I remember how absolutely fascinating and adorable my babies were. My husband was the main breadwinner, so he was not always around, but he did care for our children as much as he could. I remember when our eldest daughter was about 2 months old and became fussy in the early evening hours (as is common at that age), he was the one to figure out that if he took her outside to look at the night sky, she would calm down. I had no family living nearby to lend a hand, but fortunately, I had my husband. I also had worked with babies before and knew about laying infants down in their cribs just before fully asleep. My daughters did learn to self-soothe, and they both were able to link at least two sleep cycles together from around three months of age. I think I was able to be a more attentive and nurturing parent because I could usually get a reasonable amount of sleep at night.

All healthy babies will eventually sleep longer stretches at night, self-soothers or not. While your baby is small, enjoy the cradling and snuggling, watching him grow and learn. He will know you like having him around, encouraging him to feel good about himself. You can never get this time back again, so ultimately do what makes sense to you and feel is right, in the nurturing and tender care of your baby.

Appendices

Rules, Recommendations, and Suggestions

Rules for Better Baby Sleep

These are the hard and fast rules for infant sleep that all parents and caregivers should follow. There is a general consensus among experts, pediatricians, and public health officials for each of these rules and each one could become a life-or-death issue for your baby.

Always put babies down to sleep on their backs, and tell that to anyone else caring for them (*see page 34, Infant Sleep Safety*).

Infants should sleep on firm surfaces, ideally those designed and certified for infant sleep (*see page 34, Infant Sleep Safety*).

Infants should sleep in safe environments only (*see page 34, Infant Sleep Safety*).

Infants should never sleep on sofas, armchairs, air mattresses or waterbeds (*see page 34, Infant Sleep Safety*).

Keep pillows, fluffy comforters and sheepskins out of your baby's sleep area (*see page 34, Infant Sleep Safety*).

Mothers should not fall asleep while breast-feeding their babies (*see A Special Note for Breast-Feeding Mothers, page 24*).

If you smoke do not share a bed with your baby, do not smoke around your baby and do not smoke inside the home.

If you are using medications or substances that may impair your alertness, do not bring a baby into your bed, even for a short time (*see page 34, Infant Sleep Safety*).

Recommendations for Better Baby Sleep

These are the author's personal recommendations. Not all of these apply to every household and every baby.

Have your baby sleep in a JPMA (Juvenile Products Manufacturers Association) certified crib within monitoring distance of your bed (*see page 34, Infant Sleep Safety and Helpful Web Sites, page 68*).

Check with the CPSC (Consumer Product Safety Commission) to make sure there are no recalls out on any cribs, playpens, car seats, or any other products you use for your baby, including those purchased second hand or received as gifts (*see Helpful Web Sites, page 68*).

If you do sleep in the same bed as your baby, follow the safety tips in the section on *Maximizing Safety if You Sleep With Your Baby, page 41*.

Demand-feed your baby at first, gradually moving to a more structured type of care as the baby gets closer to four months of age (*see Don't Rush to Feed Your Baby at Night, page 22*). Socialize with your baby during the day and minimize your contact at night (*see Help Your Baby Learn the Difference Between Night and Day, page 16*).

Take your baby for daily walks outside to expose her to daylight, but not direct sunlight.

Develop a consistent, calming, and enjoyable bedtime routine (*see the section Develop a Bedtime Routine, page 20*).

Encourage your baby to learn to self-soothe to sleep by laying him down in bed a little bit awake (*see page 9, the Ability to Self-Soothe*).

Place your baby on his stomach daily, but not for sleep. Vary his positions when he is awake during the day (*see Avoiding a "Flat-Headed" Baby, page 45*).

Suggestions for Better Baby Sleep

These are ideas that may help improve your baby's sleep.

Try swaddling a newborn or fussy baby to see if this makes him more comfortable (*see Swaddling an Infant, page 18*).

Delay feeding at night, very gradually, by not rushing to feed (*see Don't Rush to Feed Your Baby at Night, page 22*).

If your baby is always waking after midnight and is hungry, try waking the baby to feed before you retire for the night.

If your baby wakes frequently at night and all his needs have been met, try moving your baby to another sleep location, from your bed to a crib, or move the crib away from the bed or to another room. You should be close enough so you can still hear your baby if they cry out for you.

Further Reading

Brazelton, T. Berry & Sparrow, Joshua D. (2003). *Sleep the Brazelton Way.* Reading, Massachusetts: Perseus Books.

Brazelton, T. Berry (1992). *Touchpoints.* Reading, Massachusetts: Perseus Books.

Cohen, G. (1999). *American Academy of Pediatrics: Guide to Your Child's Sleep.* New York: Villard Books.

Ferber, R. (2006). *Solve Your Child's Sleep Problems.* New York: Simon & Schuster.

Weissbluth, M. (2003). *Healthy Sleep Habits, Happy Child.* New York: Ballantine Books.

References

American Academy of Pediatrics Task Force on Sudden Infant Death Syndrome Policy Statement (2005). *The changing concept of sudden infant death syndrome: Diagnostic coding shifts, controversies regarding the sleep environment, and new variables to consider in reducing risk.* Pediatrics 116(5), 1245-1255.

Barr, R. (1998). *Colic and crying syndromes in infants.* Pediatrics 102.

Graham, J. (2006). *Tummy time is important.* Clinical Pediatrics 45 119-121.

Mesich, H. (2005). *Mother-infant co-sleeping.* The American Journal of Maternal Child 30(1), 30-40.

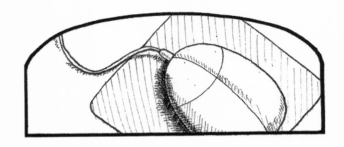

Helpful Web Sites

American Academy of Pediatrics (AAP):
> *www.aap.org*
> Healthy Child Care America
> *www.healthychildcare.org/sids.html*
> Healthy Kids Healthy Care
> *www.healthykids.us*

Centers for Disease Control & Prevention: Infants:
> *www.cdc.gov/parents/infants*

Consumer Product Safety Commission:
> *www.cpsc.gov*
> CPSC Telephone Hotline:
> 1-800-638-2772
> CPSC Crib Information Center:
> *www.cpsc.gov/cribs*

Cribs for Kids:
> *www.CribsForKids.org*

First Candle:
> *www.FirstCandle.org*

Juvenile Products Manufacturers Association:
www.jpma.org
Crib Safety:
www.CribSafety.jpma.org

National Institute of Child Health & Human Development's Back to Sleep Campaign Website:
www.nichd.nih.gov

National Resource Center for Health and Safety in Child Care and Early Education
www.nrckids.org

The National Sleep Foundation: Children & Sleep:
www.sleepfoundation.org

The National Sudden and Unexpected Infant/Child Death and Pregnancy Loss Resource Center
www.sidscenter.org

Acknowledgments

Numerous people have offered their support and assistance in developing "Better Baby Sleep." This book would not be as strong without their input. A special thank you goes to the faculty in the Family and Consumer Science Department, California State University, Northridge, and to my Parent Education colleagues at Glendale Community College. I also thank the many parents and professionals who provided thoughtful evaluations of this booklet. I am especially grateful to Carol Bloodworth, Anne Crump, Roberta Vadman and Jan Vunder, whose critical and timely feedback was invaluable.

A special acknowledgement goes to Ellen Surrey, whose illustrations make the book more inviting. I thank all of my family and friends on both sides of the Atlantic, who have always shown an interest in my work and given me constant support and encouragement, particularly my husband, Ed, and my daughters, Lauren and Katherine, who made it possible for me to write this booklet with the additional understanding of what it is like to be a mum. That is invaluable!

Disclaimer

"Better Baby Sleep" contains information intended to help parents and caregivers understand infant sleep; however, the author is not a healthcare professional and the information provided cannot substitute for the medical expertise and advice available from a pediatrician or primary healthcare provider. The author assumes no responsibility or liability for any outcomes that result after reading this book. Parents and caregivers are encouraged to discuss their infants' sleep with a qualified physician or healthcare professional.

About the Illustrator

Ellen Surrey is currently an illustration student at Art Center College of Design in Pasadena, California. Ellen's artwork is largely inspired by American culture from the 20th century, including music, movies, television, fashion, and events of the period. With her artwork Ellen hopes to evoke a nostalgic feel for the subjects depicted.

www.EllenSurrey.com

About the Author

Jane Stockly has spent her entire career working with families and children in one capacity or another, including as a nursery nurse on a maternity ward; a private nanny; a pre-school teacher; an in-home child-care provider and a parent education instructor. Born in England, Jane now resides in Southern California with her husband. She has two daughters and teaches parent education at Glendale Community College.

Webpage: *www.betterbabysleep.com*

Blog: *BetterBabySleep.blogspot.com*

Smashwords: *www.smashwords.com/profile/view/betterbabysleep*

Twitter: *BetterBabySleep*

Made in the USA
San Bernardino, CA
10 February 2015